RECEIVED

JAN 2 4 2020

Douglass-Truth Branch Library

NO LONGER PROPERTY OF
SEATTLE PUBLIC LIBRARY

D0579617

Foreword by CeCe Winans

Clap Your Hands

A Celebration of Gospel

paintings by
Michele Wood

text by
Toyomi Igus

ZONDERkidz

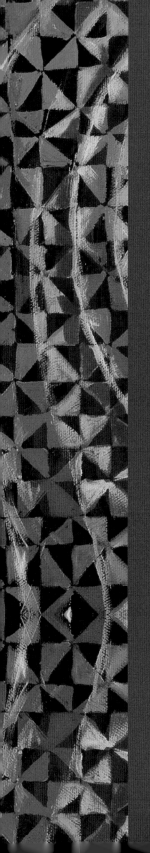

My gratitude to Michele Wood for her ennobling artistic vision; Kazumi and Kenji, my children, for nurturing my soul; and special thanks to my grandmother, Rev. Viola A. Gibson, for inspiring knowledge, faith, and cultural connection. Bless her heart.
—T.I.

To the Lord Jesus Christ, in whose name all my prayers are made, heard, and answered. To my mother, Karolyn A. Mitchell, who taught me to have hope and to believe, and through her prayers I have come to know the Lord and his Divine Art.
—M.W.

ZONDERKIDZ

Clap Your Hands
Copyright © 2019 by Toyomi Igus
Illustrations © 2019 by Michele Wood

Portions of this book were previously published with the title *I See the Rhythm of Gospel* copyright ©Toyomi Igus, Illustrations ©Michele Wood

Requests for information should be addressed to:
Zonderkidz, 3900 *Sparks Drive SE, Grand Rapids, Michigan 49546*

Hardcover ISBN 978-0-310-76947-7
Ebook ISBN 978-0-310-76949-1
Audio download ISBN 978-0310-76939-2

Any internet addresses (websites, blogs, etc.) and telephone numbers in this book are offered as a resource. They are not intended in any way to be or imply an endorsement by Zondervan, nor does Zondervan vouch for the content of these sites and numbers for the life of this book.

No part of this publication may be reproduced, stored in a retrieval system, or transmitted in any form or by any means—electronic, mechanical, photocopy, recording, or any other—except for brief quotations in printed reviews, without the prior permission of the publisher.

Zonderkidz is a trademark of Zondervan.

Editor: Annette Bourland
Design: Cindy Davis

Printed in China

19 20 21 22 23 24 25 /DSC/ 15 14 13 12 11 10 9 8 7 6 5 4 3 2 1

It is my pleasure to introduce you to the wholly unique book you now hold in your hands. Clap Your Hands is a glorious journey through the history of gospel music. Within these pages, you will see how gospel began and how it evolved over time. I know the power gospel music can have in our lives. It brings us encouragement and joy, even as we face life's challenges. It can make us feel alive!

Michele Wood's artwork captures the rich, layered history of gospel music. Toyomi Igus's poetry poignantly conveys the strength and hope that music gives us as we pull through hard times. The artists mentioned in the book have left indelible marks on the world and have been sources of inspiration for me—and others—for years. All that to say, this is a wonderfully thorough and thoughtful introduction to gospel music, and I believe you will enjoy reading it.

Each and every one of us represents the gospel of Jesus Christ. We are all living reminders of his good news, the best news. So go and sing your heart out and feel alive!

—CeCe Winans

Look for Missy, the little princess hidden inside each painting. She represents the modern-day readers, taking them back in time to engage in the rich melodies of gospel music. Look closely throughout the book and see if you can find her!
Also see additional art notes on page 40.

Clap your hands to the rhythm.
Clap your hands to the rhythm of Africa,
the motherland of humanity.
I see the rhythm of my people, land,
and spirit in harmony.

The drumbeats from our souls echo
the movement of the earth,
the journey of the sun and the mystery
of our birth.

We feel the flow of the rivers, the swing of the trees,
the migration of the birds, the tides of the seas.
We dance to the rhythm of our hearts, we sing our songs of strife,
for as creations of the creator, we are
connected to all life.

But then … in one moment …
grasping hands, clanking chains,
my voice is muffled, my family slain.

My heart is broken, my faith is shaken.
To what fearful place am I being taken?
I remember the rhythms of my homeland …
and that rhythm lives on in me.

There are many different peoples, countries, languages, and customs in Africa. The same is true of religions. Africans are Muslim, Christian, Jewish, and some still practice their native worship rituals. For all Africans, music is devotional.

1485: The Portuguese colonize the islands in the Gulf of Guinea to make sugar. But they need slaves to work the tropical plantations. This is the beginning of the slave trade; a thousand Africans a year are brought in to work the plantations.

1494: The first Africans arrive with Christopher Columbus to the West Indian island of Hispaniola (today called Haiti). They are free people.

1511: The first Africans who are slaves arrive in Hispaniola.

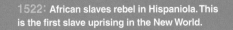 **1522:** African slaves rebel in Hispaniola. This is the first slave uprising in the New World.

From 1500–Civil War (1860s): Slaves are brought to the Caribbean Islands, the United States, and South America to provide cheap labor for landowners. About ten million Africans survive the crossing of the Atlantic Ocean, known as the Middle Passage, to the New World.

1619 : Slavery begins in the United States, when a Dutch ship steals a cargo of enslaved Africans from the Spanish. The ship arrives in Jamestown with "20 negars" to exchange for supplies. These are the first Africans to arrive in the English North American colonies.

1634 : Maryland officially adopts slavery, the first American colony of many to do so.

1642 : The Fugitive Slave Law is passed in Virginia to punish those who help enslaved people escape. Runaway slaves are branded with an "R" when they are caught.

Late 1600s : Slaves are not allowed to be educated or taught to read—even the Bible. Most Christian colonists were slave owners and discouraged the conversion of slaves to the religion. The Quakers, however, welcomed both slaves and freedmen.

6

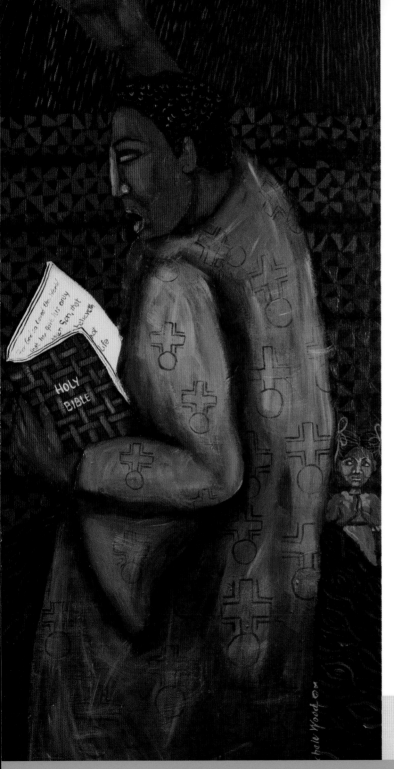

Clap your hands to the rhythm of a New World,

strange beliefs,
a life of despair,
a life of grief.

I am a motherless child, lost and confused,
trapped in the dark—used and abused.
In this new land, there are unceasing commands.

But my spirit makes new demands
of hope, home, future, salvation.

Freedom from backbreaking work and strife.
Freedom to define a new life.

But the labor beats down my body.
The hate demeans my soul.
Can I reclaim the spirit that they stole?

We find the answer in our music and in our faith
that lightens our plight.

I see the rhythm of the Americas,
as Africa's spirit shines on so bright.

Upon arrival in the new land, Africans tried to retain their tribal religious practices, but they lost them over time. They also lost their languages. At first, the enslaved blacks could not communicate well with each other, but eventually they adopted the language of the slave masters.

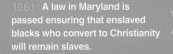
1661: A law in Maryland is passed ensuring that enslaved blacks who convert to Christianity will remain slaves.

1754: Benjamin Banneker, a 21-year-old black man, makes the first clock in colonial America, one of his many inventions.

1758: The first known black church in North America is founded, the African Baptist or "Bluestone" Church in Virginia.

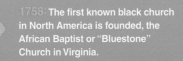
1770: Crispus Attucks, a sailor and an escaped slave, is the first civilian shot when the British attack a protesting crowd in Boston—an event known as the Boston Massacre. Attucks is the first hero of the American Revolution who died for speaking out against English rule.

Clap your hands to the rhythm of Plantation Sundays.

Shhhhh!
Quietly
we walk past the fields
we worked all week
and into the forest just beyond the creek.
Master's going to church and so are we,
but quietly, quietly.

Then we are clear—no one around. Only us to hear.
Mama hums, low and strong. Eyes closed, we hum along.
Feet shuffle, arms wave, and voices lift
our spirits higher
and higher.

Quiet no more, we clap our hands, and stomp our feet.
"Glory!" she says and "Glory!" we repeat
and repeat
as our souls fill with song and rise to greet the heavens,
the one place where we belong.

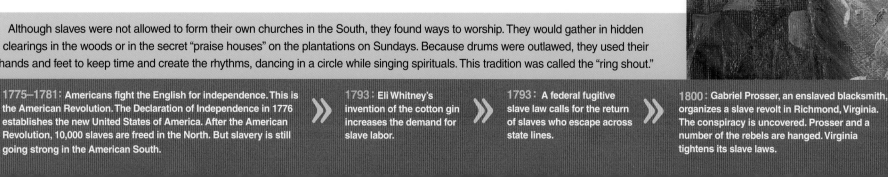

Although slaves were not allowed to form their own churches in the South, they found ways to worship. They would gather in hidden clearings in the woods or in the secret "praise houses" on the plantations on Sundays. Because drums were outlawed, they used their hands and feet to keep time and create the rhythms, dancing in a circle while singing spirituals. This tradition was called the "ring shout."

1775–1781: Americans fight the English for independence. This is the American Revolution. The Declaration of Independence in 1776 establishes the new United States of America. After the American Revolution, 10,000 slaves are freed in the North. But slavery is still going strong in the American South.

1793: Eli Whitney's invention of the cotton gin increases the demand for slave labor.

1793: A federal fugitive slave law calls for the return of slaves who escape across state lines.

1800: Gabriel Prosser, an enslaved blacksmith, organizes a slave revolt in Richmond, Virginia. The conspiracy is uncovered. Prosser and a number of the rebels are hanged. Virginia tightens its slave laws.

 1801 : The first hymnal for black churches is published, *Collection of Spiritual Songs and Hymns Selected from Various Authors*, by Richard Allen, minister of the first independent black denomination, the African Methodist Episcopal Church.

1808 : Congress stops the importation of more slaves from Africa.

 1830s : The camp meetings that start the Second Great Awakening are popular. Both blacks and whites flock to these revival meetings, where many are converted to Christianity. Often whites sing with the black slaves.

1831: Nat Turner leads seventy fellow slaves in a two-day rebellion in Virginia, killing sixty whites. The same year, William Lloyd Garrison begins publishing *The Liberator*, a weekly newspaper that calls for the abolition of slavery. Later, former slave Frederick Douglass joins Garrison's antislavery movement.

1840s: People of the northern and southern states become increasingly divided over slavery. The issue also divides religious communities. In 1840, southern Methodists cannot agree with northern Methodists about the morality of slavery.

1847: Former slave Frederick Douglass launches his abolitionist newspaper, *The North Star*.

Clap your hands to the rhythm of our hope

for freedom in the Promised Land
on the face of Brother Otis as he takes my sister's hand
and they run.

Swiftly.
Silently.
I see them mouth their goodbyes
with tears in their eyes,
slinking past our shacks,
taking one quick look back
to wave at me.

I watch their night shadows as, bodies fueled by fear,
they run through the fields hoping the dogs won't hear
their hearts pounding in their ears
or their feet slapping through the muddy banks of the river.

When they step into the water, my sister gives a shiver.
Brother Otis holds her tighter,
knowing that the river will deliver

them to FREEDOM.

Former slave Harriet Tubman helped other slaves escape through the "Underground Railroad" to freedom in the North, moving secretly from town to town. They were helped along the way by abolitionists, people who opposed slavery.

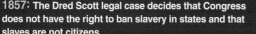 **1857:** The Dred Scott legal case decides that Congress does not have the right to ban slavery in states and that slaves are not citizens.

 1861: The Civil War between the northern and southern states begins.

 1863: President Abraham Lincoln issues the Emancipation Proclamation, declaring "that all persons held as slaves" will be free.

Clap your hands to the rhythm of jubilee day,

shining in the hopeful faces of my family as we make our way
north to find our new home.
Our wagon is packed with food, quilts,
our personal things,
not quite sure where we're going or how much to bring,
and to pass the time away, our people hum and sing
our old spirituals.

"We free now, baby," Mama whispers as we
bounce and sway
with the wagon's twists and turns over roads of clay
through the land that oppressed us
to a new world, a brand-new day.
Free.

We waited so long to say that word;
we thought our prayers would never be heard.
But what is free? What does that mean?
Am I free to be me? Will I ever be seen?

Or will their faces always turn mean when we arrive on the scene?
I see the rhythm of our emancipation
in the songs sung by freed men who are still not free.

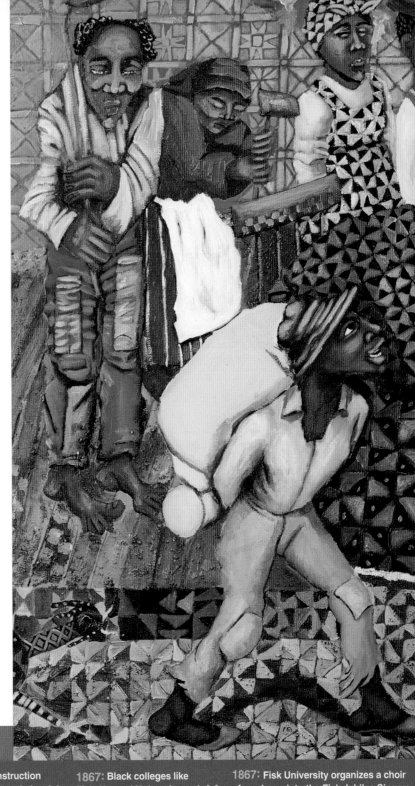

In 1865, slavery was abolished in America. This day of liberation is called Day of Jubilee.

1865: Congress establishes the Freedmen's Bureau to protect the rights of newly freed blacks. The Civil War ends; President Lincoln is assassinated; and the Ku Klux Klan is formed by ex-Confederates.

1865–1866: The "Black Codes" are passed by southern states. These laws try to drastically restrict the rights of newly freed slaves.

1866–1877: The Reconstruction Era begins. Congress attempts to reorganize the states devastated by the Civil War and establish a non-slave society.

1867: Black colleges like Fisk, Howard University, and Morehouse start to graduate a new generation of black leaders.

1867: Fisk University organizes a choir of ex-slaves into the Fisk Jubilee Singers. Groups like this popularize the old African-American spirituals worldwide when they tour and perform.

1868: The Fourteenth Amendment to the Constitution states that individuals born in the United States are American citizens, including those born as slaves.

1870: The Fifteenth Amendment to the Constitution gives black men the right to vote.

1877: Attempts by the government to provide basic civil rights for blacks quickly erode after Reconstruction ends.

1879–1880: The Black Exodus takes place. Tens of thousands of African Americans migrate from southern states to Kansas to find a better life.

1882–1930: Over 3,700 men and women are reported lynched or hanged. Most are southern blacks. Lynching is a tactic used by southern racists to brutalize and intimidate black people.

1896 : The Supreme Court decision *Plessy v. Ferguson* says that racial segregation is constitutional. This decision allows the Jim Crow laws in the South to take hold. These laws kept blacks oppressed after the Civil War.

1907 : Madame C. J. Walker builds a beauty products empire developing hair care products for black women. She becomes the first African-American millionaire.

1909 : The National Association for the Advancement of Colored People (NAACP) is founded by black and white intellectuals and led by W. E. B. Du Bois. It becomes the most influential black civil rights organization in America, dedicated to political equality and social justice.

Clap your hands to the rhythm
in the sanctified churches
of black folk who flock to the pews
after days of doing hard jobs white folks don't want to do.

Every Sunday morning, in the California heat,
I follow the grown-ups down to meet
all the friends and neighbors hurrying to get a seat
at Azusa Street.
There I watch as Pastor Seymour preaches and beseeches
us to feel the spirit.

Then, one by one, the grown-ups stand and testify about His commands.
Their bodies shake, their voices lift and shout.
I get a little nervous as I look about and see
the people I know move in some strange dance,
speaking in tongues, falling in a trance …
"Amen!" the preacher yells. "Amen!" we say.
"Hallelujah!" "Hallelujah!"

This goes on all day, until, one by one, they each surrender
to experience some ecstatic splendor
that leaves them refreshed and soft and tender
ready to start a new week.
I see the rhythm at Azusa Street,
when the spirit rises and starts to speak.

To escape the south, African-Americans also migrated west. At 312 Azusa Street, Los Angeles, California, the Pentecostal movement is believed to have been born.

 1909: Admiral Robert E. Peary, African-American Matthew Henson, and four Inuit scouts become the first men to reach the North Pole.

1914: Marcus Garvey establishes the Universal Negro Improvement Association, an influential black nationalist organization "to promote the spirit of race pride" and create a sense of worldwide unity among blacks.

 1917: The United States joins the Allied Forces in World War I.

Clap your hands to the rhythm of Bronzeville

on Chicago's South Side,
where black folk come together to create, reside,
and build a community full of love and pride.

For a while, we are fine,
we look forward to more,
but after Black Tuesday, we become more poor—
Papa loses his job to the man next door—
and Mama has to cook and start cleaning floors.

We find escape through our artists, who make jazz and blues so fine—
Louis Armstrong, Bessie Smith,
Ethel Waters, Fatha Hines—
and in our churches, we start to hear the same rhythm lines
when the Father of Gospel makes new music that shines on and on.

"Precious Lord, take my hand," he wrote when she died.
"Precious Lord, take my hand," he sings and we cry.
I see the rhythms of Thomas Dorsey and his choirs
who made music that inspires
all of us who are so, so tired.

Like New York's Harlem Renaissance, Chicago's South Side in the 1920s and '30s was also a center of African-American creativity in an area called "Bronzeville." Thomas Dorsey, known as the Father of Gospel, moved to Chicago to join the exciting blues and jazz scene as a performer. It was while he attended a National Baptist Convention there that he was inspired to create a unique gospel music. He added blues and jazz elements to religious hymns, creating the choral gospel blues.

1921: African-American Bessie Coleman becomes the first woman to receive an international pilot's license to fly.

At the 1921 National Baptist Convention, evangelist W. M. Nix is invited to preach and promote the *Gospel Pearls* hymnal—the first publication by a black congregation to use the term "gospel."

1923: The famous Cotton Club opens in Harlem.

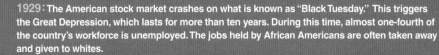
1929 : The American stock market crashes on what is known as "Black Tuesday." This triggers the Great Depression, which lasts for more than ten years. During this time, almost one-fourth of the country's workforce is unemployed. The jobs held by African Americans are often taken away and given to whites.

1932 : Thomas Dorsey's wife and son die in childbirth. In his grief, he writes "Take My Hand, Precious Lord," one of the world's most popular gospel songs.

1931: Nine black youths are charged with raping two white women in Scottsboro, Alabama. Although there is little evidence, the southern jury sentences them to death. The Supreme Court overturns their convictions twice. In a third trial, four of the Scottsboro boys are freed; but five are sentenced to long prison terms.

 1934: Harlem's famous Apollo Theater opens.

 1934: In this year, eight gospel quartets record their music. By 1939, every major record label is recording at least one gospel quartet.

 1936: African-American track star Jesse Owens wins four gold medals at the Berlin Olympics.

Clap your hands to the rhythm of gospel quartets

in the soulful voices heard on our radio set.
Soul Stirrers, Pilgrim Travelers, Dixie Hummingbirds
record their a cappella harmonies to spread the word
of the gospel.

When the Golden Gate Quartet comes to our town,
me and June Bug run around
trying to find a way to hear their sound.

"Shoo!" says the ticket taker when we try to slide by.
"Get outta here!" says the guard when we sneak in on the sly.
So we climb on up that big sycamore tree,
and we perch ourselves out on a limb to see
the Quartet in all their finery.

For the next hour, me and June Bug, caught up in the stories,
pretend to be Bible heroes in their tales of glory,
Joshua and the battle, Jonah and the whale,
Sampson, Job, and Noah, Ezekiel, and Gabriel.
I see the rhythm of gospel in these happy harmonies
that never fail.

Thomas Dorsey's new gospel sound did not immediately become popular among African Americans because his style was not accepted by many churches and his music was not recorded. However, gospel quartets—like the Golden Gate Quartet shown here—quickly became famous due to their recordings and radio play. Like barbershop quartets, black religious quartets sang in rich harmonies.

1939: Because she is black, famous opera singer Marian Anderson is forbidden to perform at Constitution Hall in Washington, D.C., by the Daughters of the American Revolution. She instead performs on the steps of the Lincoln Memorial on Easter Day, drawing an audience of 75,000 people.

1941: President Franklin Roosevelt and his wife, Eleanor, invite the Golden Gate Quartet to perform at Constitution Hall. This time the Daughters of the American Revolution do not object.

1941: Pearl Harbor, Hawaii, is attacked on December 7th by Japanese forces. On December 8th, the United States enters World War II.

1941: The Tuskegee Institute establishes its first pilot training program for blacks. The Tuskegee Airmen—black pilots who trained there—fight heroically for the United States in World War II.

19

Clap your hands to the rhythm of gospel women

hugging you, hugging me, hugging Him,
caring for our people, hearts filled to the brim.
(*When I grow up, I want to be just like them.*)

With sanctified voices—powerful and strong—
our gospel divas channel His love through song:
Queen Mahalia moves us up a little higher,
The Cotton Club finds Sister Tharpe in swing.
Pastor Shirley preaches with the choir,
shouting and telling stories before she starts to sing.

Gospel women turn city streets into sacred spaces,
recording studios into holy places.
They pull us up out of gutters and into the pews
to ease our burden and bring us good news,
mixing the message of salvation
with the rhythms of the blues.

Gospel women make music that shows
He's got the whole world in His hands,
turning our earthly sorrows
into hopes for the promised land.
I feel the loving rhythms of our gospel mothers
creating music that feels like home.

Black women have always been strong supporters of the black church. Despite the lack of opportunities in a world run by men, black women made their mark in America. In religious circles and in the larger entertainment world, there are many notable female gospel singers.

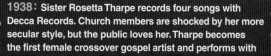

1935: Mary McLeod Bethune, the daughter of slaves, founder of the Bethune-Cookman College, and advisor to President Roosevelt, starts the National Council of Negro Women, bringing together the leaders of twenty-eight women's organizations.

1938: Sister Rosetta Tharpe records four songs with Decca Records. Church members are shocked by her more secular style, but the public loves her. Tharpe becomes the first female crossover gospel artist and performs with

1941–45: A second wave of southern blacks migrates north and west to provide labor for the war industry. Gospel singer Roebuck "Pops" Staples and his family are part of this movement. They move from Mississippi to Chicago to work in the meatpacking plants. The

1948: Mahalia Jackson's "Move on Up a Little Higher" sells over two million copies, making her the Queen of Gospel.

1950: Mahalia Jackson brings gospel to Carnegie Hall. Her popularity increases as she is featured as one of the first African Americans on national television.

1950: Poet Gwendolyn Brooks becomes the first African American to win a Pulitzer Prize.

1955: While touring in South Carolina, Shirley Caesar's entourage stops at a gas station to buy drinks. Shirley's crew is attacked by the gas station owner and his attendants. Several members of her group are beaten with hammers and bottles. Shirley escapes unharmed.

1945: World War II ends with the surrender of Germany and Japan.

1947: Jackie Robinson is signed to the Brooklyn Dodgers, becoming the first black man to play major league baseball.

1948: President Harry S. Truman issues an order to integrate the U.S. armed forces. Before this order, black and white American soldiers fought separately in segregated military units.

1950: African-American scholar and U.S. diplomat Ralph Bunche is the first person of color to win the Nobel Peace Prize for his work in negotiating an Arab-Israeli truce in Palestine.

Clap your hands to the rhythm of the gospel highway,

getting stronger as radio stations start to play
more and more of our music every day.

Gospel quartets and choirs—now much in demand—
travel from town to town to sing and shake hands
with the crowd.

I watch our famous singers, who perform to standing ovations,
get shuffled off to the colored sections of trains at the station.
"With these Jim Crow laws, we might as well be back on the plantation,"
Brother William grumbles with frustration.
(*See, Brother William just got home from the war*
and he—like other black men—were really pretty sore
that the country they fought for did not respect them more.)

So when gospel singers come to perform in our town,
Mama offers our home so they can rest, lie down,
and enjoy a good home-cooked meal (best cornbread around!).

I see the rhythm of the gospel highway in the warm, grateful faces of the singers who show up at our door.

After World War II, many new record companies emerged, recording more gospel music. Gospel singers performed in churches, community centers, and auditoriums across the country. This network of venues was called "the gospel highway." Because of discrimination, blacks were not allowed to stay in most hotels or eat in most restaurants and had to travel in the poor third-class sections of trains and buses. The more successful singers traveled in their own buses and cars, but often encountered racism during their tours.

1950: Sam Cooke joins the Soul Stirrers, pushing them to the top of their careers. Cooke goes on to become one of the most notable gospel singers to successfully cross over into secular music.

1954: In the case of *Brown v. Board of Education of Topeka, Kansas*, the Supreme Court rules that segregation in public schools is unconstitutional. After this ruling, schools start to become integrated. The case was argued and won by African-American attorney Thurgood Marshall.

Clap your hands to the rhythm of our lament

as people of all races sing our discontent
through gospel's Freedom Songs.

The Staples demand, "Respect yourself!"
"That's enough," wails Dorothy Coates.
"People get ready," warns Curtis Mayfield
with his uplifting falsetto notes.
The voices of the people start to fly,
and "We Shall Overcome" becomes the movement's battle cry.

I see the passion of the students who come into our town
to convince us we must stand our ground.
"Register to vote, fight for your rights,
don't settle for less, get up and unite!"

My mother takes a deep breath, clears out her throat,
combs back her hair, puts on her coat,
and says, "It's time, I'm registering to vote."

My father, in silence, looks at her with pride,
then he puts on his hat and stands by her side,
and I watch them leave together, my eyes open wide.
I see the rhythm of the Freedom Songs and
I have a dream.

The Civil Rights Movement of the 1960s brought attention to the fact that, even a hundred years after slavery was outlawed, blacks were not yet treated as equal American citizens.

1955: A young black boy, Emmett Till, is brutally killed for allegedly whistling at a white woman in Mississippi. Two white men charged with his murder are acquitted by an all-white jury. They later boast about killing the boy. The public outrage helps the Civil Rights Movement.

1955: Rosa Parks is arrested for refusing to give up her bus seat to a white passenger. In response, Montgomery, Alabama's black community launches a successful year-long bus boycott.

1957: Although ordered by the Federal government to allow the students in, nine black youths are blocked from entering Central High School in Little Rock, Arkansas. Federal troops and the National Guard intervene on behalf of the students, who become known as the "Little Rock Nine."

1961: Over the spring and summer, 1,000 white and black student volunteers begin taking bus trips through the South to test new laws prohibiting segregation in bus and railway stations. They are called "freedom riders."

1963: Dr. Martin Luther King Jr. delivers his famous "I Have a Dream" speech at the March on Washington for Jobs and Freedom, which is attended by about 250,000 people.

1963: The Sixteenth Street Baptist Church in Birmingham, Alabama, is bombed, killing four little girls.

1964: President Lyndon Johnson signs the Civil Rights Act, prohibiting discrimination of all kinds based on race, color, religion, or national origin.

1964: Dr. King receives the Nobel Peace Prize.

1962 : James Cleveland records "Peace Be Still" with the First Baptist Church Choir, which sells 800,000 copies. He becomes a superstar overnight.

1965–1970 : Americans actively protest the United States' involvement in the Vietnam War.

1965 : Congress passes the Voting Rights Act of 1965, making it easier for southern blacks to register to vote.

1965 : In six days of rioting in Los Angeles, thirty-five people are killed and almost 1,000 injured.

1967 : Major race riots also take place in Newark and Detroit.

Clap your hands to the rhythms of exploration,

a time of open minds, fairer laws, and innovation.
We put a man on the moon, up in outer space—
from where he stands he can see no face, no trace
of any single person—only one planet, one place.

But back on Earth that still is not the case.
(*I wonder what it's like not to see race.*)
I see riots in my city—too many drugs and guns.

Although we now have equal rights, there's still work to be done.
But … on the TV and radio, there is an exciting change:
the rhythms of rock, pop, and soul combine, exchange,
and broaden the range of gospel music.

Bradford brings gospel to the Broadway stage.
Hawkins' "Oh Happy Day" becomes all the rage.
Crouch finds new audiences to engage.
Cleveland's foot-stompin' choir music comes of age.

These fathers of modern gospel create new voices so that
black, white, young, old now have choices of joyous, uplifting music.

In the 1960s and '70s, American culture started to reflect the diversity of its people. Black musical genres like rhythm and blues and soul became hugely popular all over the world. Gospel was also introduced by these styles of music—and the line between gospel and secular music became blurred.

1967 : Attorney and civil rights leader Thurgood Marshall becomes the first black Supreme Court Justice.

1968 : Dr. Martin Luther King Jr. is assassinated in Memphis, Tennessee.

1975 : Morehouse School of Medicine is established—the only black medical school in the United States.

1977 : The Apple II computer is introduced, revolutionizing the personal home computer.

27

Clap your hands to the rhythms of Motown and funk

in the new pop-gospel music of our time.
The smoothness of the music makes us sway to the beat,
the bass lines make us want to jump to our feet,
and its popularity moves it from the church to the street.

Nana and the old folks complain every day:
"Real gospel music can't be sung that way.
And gospel at the Apollo? Just ain't right," they'd say.
"Gospel should have that old Dorsey feel."
But to us Al Green, Tramaine, and the Winans were ideal.

I never understood why the old folks complained.
If the music spread the word, then it wasn't in vain.
Can't gospel music inspire and entertain?
Besides, the music was more fun than listening to them explain
how things were back in their day!
I see the rhythm of gospel soul reach out and speak to a new generation.

There were many contempory gospel stars in the 1980s, but one family is credited as being the biggest influence on gospel music in that decade—the Winans.

 1985: Black artists BeBe and CeCe Winans sign with Christian record label, Sparrow Records.

 1985: Youth minister Stephen Wiley releases the first full-length Christian rap album, *Bible Break*.

 1986: January 20th is officially designated Martin Luther King Jr. Day, a national holiday.

29

1990 : South African activist Nelson Mandela is freed after spending twenty-seven years in prison for fighting against the racist apartheid laws of his country.

1991: Gospel Music Association adds a rap/hip-hop album category to its Dove Music Awards.

1992 : The Los Angeles policemen on trial for the beating of an African-American man, Rodney King, are acquitted. The acquittal ignites civil disorder in communities of color in Los Angeles.

1992 : Dr. Mae Jemison becomes the first African-American woman in space.

Clap your hands to the rhythm
of gospel music power

moving the word through television, internet, and radio,

and on the stages of our megachurches where they echo and flow

into the hearts of thousands.

Donnie urges me to get up when I fall down.

Soulful Yolanda crafts her music with a slick, urban sound.

Kirk and the Family's crossover gospel is the best around.

Tye Tribbett takes chances and explores new ground.

(I really like his more hip-hoppy sound.)

We young people love the music, but it surely confounds

our elders.

Our singers are superstars; our ministers, celebrities.

The power of their performances makes us want to drop to our knees and pray,

Please! Help us in our journey to live a better way.

I hear the rhythm of my childhood plight

in music that helps me understand what's wrong, what's right,

that teaches me how to live a life that is contrite

and full of love that is divinely bright.

The 1990s saw the rise of the black urban "megachurches," where thousands of worshipers could gather for one service. The popularity of gospel music prompted the birth of a gospel music cable television station, magazine, and music awards, yet the message of the music continued to rise above the commercialism. New voices, such as that of Donnie McClurkin and Kirk Franklin, engaged many young people who were still negatively affected by poverty, drugs, broken families, poor schools, and the lack of social services.

 1993: Toni Morrison becomes the first African American to win the Nobel Prize in Literature for her novel, *Beloved*.

 1994: Nelson Mandela is elected the first black president of South Africa in the country's first free elections. Apartheid is officially over.

1995: The Million Man March is organized in Washington, D.C., to affirm collective responsibility among African Americans and to protest the violence, drugs, and unemployment affecting black men.

 1998: The body of James Byrd Jr. is found. He was lynched in Jasper, Texas, by three white men.

Like the blues, jazz, rhythm-and-blues, and soul styles of earlier years, hip-hop also influenced gospel. Cross Movement, Tye Tribbett, Lecrae, and Da T.R.U.T.H. are only a few of the many musicians who used rap and hip-hop styles to reach the youth of the 21st century with positive inspirational messages and stories of finding salvation through Jesus Christ.

Clap your hands to the rhythm of holy hip-hop,

rising from the alleys and the urban underground,
speaking to me with familiar sounds.
I see the rhythms reflecting my life,
my hopelessness, struggle, pain, and strife,
trying to find meaning and purpose for my soul,
a map for my journey, a hand up out of the hole.

But the world I see
on internet and TV
doesn't speak to me.
It is not my family's life of bounced rent checks
or drugs and violence in the projects.
The world just seems far too complex,
and I don't have many choices.

Then I hear the holy message through the hip-hop rhythms,
those rappin' rhythms that release the tension,
exposing painful memories I dare not mention,
opening spaces in my heart to receive comprehension
that there is a different life, a new dimension
for people like me.
**I see the rhythm and hope in hip-hop gospel,
and the rhythm lives on in me.**

2001: On September 11th, al-Qaeda terrorists hijack and crash four commercial airplanes into the World Trade Center, the Pentagon, and a field in Pennsylvania, killing almost 3,000

2001: African-Americans General Colin L. Powell and Condoleezza Rice are appointed to President Bush's cabinet. General Powell becomes secretary of state, and Condoleezza

» **2003:** In *Grutter v. Bollinger*, the Supreme Court rules that race can be one of the factors considered by colleges when selecting their students because it furthers "a compelling interest in obtaining the educational benefits that flow from a diverse student body."

» **2005:** Hurricane Katrina devastates the Gulf Coast. The black communities are hit the hardest.

» **2008:** African-American Illinois senator Barack Obama is elected the 44th president of the United States.

2008: The United States formally apologizes to black Americans for slavery and the later Jim Crow laws that continued to discriminate against African Americans.

2009: The animated movie *The Princess and the Frog* features the first African-American Disney princess, Tiana.

2012: Seventeen-year-old Trayvon Martin, while walking in his father's neighborhood, is killed by a white Florida man who claimed to be on neighborhood watch. The subsequent acquittal of Trayvon's killer spurs outrage in the African-American community, leading to the start of the #BlackLivesMatter movement.

2015: Nine African-American church-goers are killed by a white supremacist during a prayer service at the Emanuel African Methodist Episcopal Church in downtown Charleston, South Carolina.

Clap your hands to the rhythm of urban gospel

as we sit in Sunday service and grieve another young man.
I see the rhythm of soulful gospel
and pray to stop the violence and hatred rising over the land.
There's a healing in this room, Sister Tasha sings out.
I'm gonna put a praise on it!
And we answer with a joyful shout,
feeling comforted and healed as we all file out
of the church.

Until another post, another tweet, won't let me forget
that there's no justice, no peace for us … not yet.
We all bleed the same
So tell me why, tell me why
We're divided.
Then I hear the voices of our young gospel singers—
Mandisa who lifts our hearts, our hopes up high,
Brother Travis and his guitar singing love's battle cry.
My soul draws strength from their words
and I know that by and by
Love will prevail.
I see the rhythm of a world that's free
so let's clap our hands to those rhythms created for you and me
Equally.

The presidential election of Barack Obama was a hopeful sign that America finally had moved into an era of racial acceptance. However, despite the growing tolerance for diversity, the words and actions of many public figures—witnessed by millions through social media—show that ethnic, religious, and gender biases are still embedded in American culture. In music, the diversity of secular musical styles is embraced by new gospel singers and musicians, like Travis Greene and Tasha Cobb Leonard. The black church remains a sanctuary of support and empowerment for many African-American communities.

2016: *Billboard* issues its first Gospel Music Award to Kirk Franklin.

2016: Colin Kaepernick, a San Francisco 49ers' football quarterback, kneels in protest of racial injustice and police killings while the U.S. National Anthem is played during his games. He is subsequently released from the team and is not hired by any other National Football League team.

2017: A neo-Nazi attending a white supremacist rally in Charlottesville, North Carolina, attacks peaceful protestors with his car, causing the death of one young woman and injuring several others.

2018: African-American leaders, celebrities, and churches join other immigration activists in Washington, D.C. to protest the Trump administration's immigration policies.

The themes of African-American gospel songs are often drawn from Bible stories. This picture is an illustration of the prophetess Miriam leading Hebrew women in song and dance, celebrating the Exodus of the Hebrew slaves and the defeat of the Egyptians. Gospel music also reflects the natural world and personal experiences of African Americans.

Author Note

Gospel evolved from the early African-American spiritual, but no one can say exactly when and where the spiritual got its start. Did enslaved Africans copy and change the European Christian and folk music? Did they bring their own African religious songs to the New World and modify them? Or did enslaved Africans create their own unique songs? Historians are still asking these questions. What we do know is that the African-American spiritual was born out of the brutality of slavery and evolved into what we know today as "gospel music."

In the original version of this book, the timeline ended on a joyful note with the election of America's first black president. Despite that major achievement, African Americans—and all minority groups in our country—still face bigotry, hatred, and violence. But our response is always the same—to love and keep the faith.

It is through gospel music that many of us express the pain and sorrow of life's many challenges. It is also through gospel music that souls are uplifted, strengthened, and inspired.

The good news is that African Americans and our unique culture have not only survived, we've thrived! And the good news is gospel.

—Toyomi Igus

Illustrator Note

Back in 2004, my intentions were to honor our dear sweet Lord Jesus, when I presented the concept for this book (previously titled *I See the Rhythm of Gospel*) to Toyomi Igus. Since then, I continued to believe in God's *gift from above* that was given to me, and now we have an extended version of the book. I feel jubilant that CeCe Winans has written the foreword, as it was her DVD *Live in the Throne Room* that was an inspiration to me. I sold the DVD back when I was working in the music department of a Christian bookstore, and this is how I met a Voice of the Lord.

It is my hope that this updated edition shows readers that gospel music is important for the Christian faith and prevailing through praise and worship. More than anything, gospel music points to the Word. The gospel of John begins, "In the beginning was the Word, and the Word was with God, and the Word was God." The lyrics of the praise and worship songs incorporate "the Word" and reveal a character trait about the Lord Jesus. For He is holy and worthy of praise. This book is my joy of praise. May you learn and grow to give the Lord a Hallelujah Praise!

—Michele Wood

Discography

Here are some gospel songs representing different eras in African-American gospel history. Listen to these as you start your exploration of gospel music.

Africa: "Ke Na Le Modisa"—Soweto Gospel Choir

New World—The Great Awakening: "Swing Low, Sweet Chariot" or "Nobody Knows the Trouble I Seen"—traditional gospel songs that have been sung by various artists

Plantation Sundays: "Run Old Jeremiah: Echoes of the Ring Shout"—you can find a good sample of a ring shout sung by Joe Washington Brown and Austin Coleman in 1934 at historymatters.gmu.edu/d/5759/

Our Hope—The Promised Land: "Go Down, Moses" or "Steal Away"—traditional gospel songs that have been sung by various artists

Jubilee Day: "I'm on the Battlefield for My Lord"—The Fisk Jubilee Singers

Sanctified Churches: "We'll Understand It Better By and By"—Charles Tindley

Bronzeville: "Take My Hand, Precious Lord"—Thomas Dorsey

Gospel Quartets: "Lord I've Tried"—Soul Stirrers; "Ezekiel Saw the Wheel"—Golden Gate Quartet

Gospel Women: "He's Got the Whole World in His Hands"—Mahalia Jackson; "Jesus, I Love Calling Your Name" —Shirley Caesar; "Didn't It Rain"—Rosetta Tharpe

Gospel Highway: "Jesus Gave Me Water"—Sam Cooke; "The Lord's Prayer"—Five Blind Boys of Mississippi

Our Lament—The Civil Rights Movement: "We Shall Overcome"—the American civil rights anthem

Exploration—Fathers of Modern Gospel: "Jesus is the Answer"—Andraé Crouch; "Oh Happy Day"—Edwin Hawkins; "Peace Be Still"—James Cleveland

Gospel Soul—Motown and Funk: "I'll Take You There"—BeBe and CeCe Winans; "Wherever You Are"—Yolanda Adams

Gospel Power: "Why We Sing"—Kirk Franklin; "Stand"—Donnie McClurkin; "No Way"—Tye Tribbett

Holy Hip-Hop: "Holy Culture"—Cross Movement; "Take Me As I Am"—Lecrae; "Who Am I?"—Da T.R.U.T.H.

Urban Gospel: "Made A Way"—Travis Greene; "Unfinished"—Mandisa; "Blessings"—Chance the Rapper

Discussion Questions

1. *Clap Your Hands* presents African-American history through the evolution of gospel music from the beginning of slavery to the present day. Which parts of history were you already familiar with? Which parts were new to you? What did you learn about African-American history?

2. Gospel music served as the basis for other musical genres, such as blues, jazz, rap, and hip-hop. What do these different genres have in common? How are they different from one another? What's your favorite kind of music and why?

3. A timeline runs throughout the book, detailing important events that occurred during each time period. How does this contribute to your understanding of the book?

4. *Clap Your Hands* is written as a series of poems. Why do you think the author chose to do this? Do you see a connection between poetry and music?

5. The book includes a discography of important gospel songs throughout history. Look up one of the songs online and listen to it. How would you describe the song? What emotions does it convey? How does it fit in with the book?

Further Reading List

Andrews, Troy. *The 5 O'Clock Band*. Illustrated by Bryan Collier. New York: Abrams Books for Young Readers, 2018.

Andrews, Troy. *Trombone Shorty*. Illustrated by Bryan Collier. New York: Abrams Books for Young Readers, 2015.

Clark-Robinson, Monica. *Let the Children March*. Illustrated by Frank Morrison. New York: Houghton Mifflin Harcourt, 2018.

Grady, Cynthia. *Like a Bird: The Art of the American Slave Song*. Illustrated by Michele Wood. Minneapolis: Millbrook Press, 2016.

Hill, Laban Carrick. *When the Beat Was Born: DJ Kool Herc and the Creation of Hip Hop*. Illustrated by Theodore Taylor III. New York: Roaring Brook Press, 2013.

Russell-Brown, Katheryn. *Little Melba and Her Big Trombone*. Illustrated by Frank Morrison. New York: Lee & Low Books, 2014.

Tonatiuh, Duncan. *Separate Is Never Equal: Sylvia Mendez and Her Family's Fight for Desegregation*. New York: Abrams Books for Young Readers, 2014.

Weatherford, Carole Boston. *Freedom in Congo Square*. Illustrated by R. Gregory Christie. New York: Little Bee Books, 2016.

Weatherford, Carole Boston. *The Roots of Rap: 16 Bars on the 4 Pillars of Hip-Hop*. Illustrated by Frank Morrison. New York: Little Bee Books, 2019.

Art Descriptions

Pgs 4–5: In this picture, the first panel shows a woman washing clothes in the river, while African villagers are being captured by European slavers. The dye leaking into the river from the ends of the two red scarves represents the blood shed by African people who died in the slave trade. Many West African tribes had customs similar to baptism, which the water of the river represents. The center panel shows villagers dancing and drumming in celebration. Some tribes believe that the spirits are summoned with the drumming.

Pgs 6–7: Jesus is shown here as one of the slaves, illustrating how, even though the Bible was used to justify slavery, Jesus suffered on behalf of all mankind. The minister on the right preaches at a plantation revival meeting. These meetings provide comfort to the hardworking slaves. The conversion of slaves to Christianity in the 1700s is called the Great Awakening.

Pgs 10–11: Here, the red and white stripes and maple leaf on Harriet's skirt symbolize the flag of Canada. It is believed that Tubman used spirituals as signals to slaves preparing for escape. The spiritual "Wade in the Water" instructed slaves how to throw the slave trackers' bloodhounds off their scent by walking through water.

Pgs 12–13: The image shows newly freed slaves moving north to freedom and hopeful prosperity. The books represent the opportunities blacks now had for education. The church symbolizes how black churches became safe havens for African Americans as they settled into their new communities.

Pgs 14–15: In this picture, people at this Azusa Street revival meeting feel "the Spirit" and are encouraged to "testify," that is, speak, sing, and dance spontaneously about their faith. Much of African-American gospel music has it roots in these "sanctified" or Pentecostal churches.

Pgs 16–17: Here, Dorsey leads a gospel chorus at Ebenezer Baptist Church in Chicago.

Pgs 20–21: This painting is a tribute to three performers: Mahalia Jackson, Sister Rosetta Tharpe, and Shirley Caesar.

Pgs 24–25: Here, black university students stage a "sit-in" at a Woolworth's lunch counter, peacefully protesting the fact that blacks cannot be served food there. Behind them, sanitation workers march for basic employment rights. The guards represent the National Guard troops who were sent by President Kennedy to protect the protesters. At the bottom, people are lined up to register to vote for the first time.

Pgs 26–27: In the background of this picture, you can see the faces of some of the gospel innovators of this time (from left to right): Edwin Hawkins, Sam Cooke, James Cleveland, Thomas Dorsey, Andrae Crouch, Rance Allen, and Alex Bradford. The choir leader is James Cleveland, who developed the modern black gospel choir style.

Pgs 28–29: Here, brother and sister BeBe (right) and CeCe Winans (left) are singing at Harlem's Apollo Theater. Over the course of the 1960s to the '80s, two branches of gospel music developed: contemporary gospel, which reached a wide secular audience, and traditional gospel, which was still extremely popular.